THE JOY OF

JUGGLING

DAVE FINNIGAN
AKA "PROFESSOR CONFIDENCE"

ILLUSTRATED BY BRUCE EDWARDS

TECHNICAL CONSULTANT: ALLEN JACOBS

JUGGLEBUG

THE JOY OF JUGGLING

JUGGLEBUG, March 1993
Fully Revised Second Edition

Published in the United States by Jugglebug, 7526J Olympic View Dr.
Edmonds, WA 98026. (206) 774-2127

Illustration and layout by Bruce Edwards, Magigraphics

Library of Congress Catalog Card Number 93-091392
Finnigan, Dave
The Joy of Juggling
JUGGLEBUG
I. Jugglers and Juggling.
II. Games
III. Title
ISBN 0-9615521-3-1

Manufactured in the United States of America

The Joy of Juggling

by Dave Finnigan
Illustrated by Bruce Edwards

Table of Contents

Author's Preface

In 1979 JUGGLEBUG published *The Joy of Juggling*. Since then over 200,000 copies of that 38 page book have been bought by folks eager to learn enough juggling to put on a little show. *The Joy of Juggling* presented a dozen 3 ball tricks, using 43 illustrations, about one month's worth of "homework" for a beginning juggler.

In 1987 JUGGLEBUG published *The Complete Juggler*, an encyclopedia of juggling lore, with over 1,000 illustrations. *The Complete Juggler* updated much of the material in *The Joy of Juggling*. *The Complete Juggler* goes far beyond 3 balls, covering 4, 5, 6, and 7 balls, rings, clubs, partner work, and the more esoteric items in the juggler's prop bag, diabolos, devil sticks, cigar boxes, spinning plates, top hats, and spinning balls. It includes an extensive chapter on the history of juggling and lesson plans for teachers; but at 576 pages it is more of a commitment than some folks are willing to make to a new hobby.

So now we are publishing a fully revised edition of *The Joy of Juggling*. It includes two dozen ball tricks, information on starting out with slow moving nylon scarves, how to move on to rings and clubs, and 190 detailed illustrations. This book more than triples the scope of it's predecessor and should provide you with enough material to stay busy for several months. Then if you have been bitten by the Jugglebug you can get a copy of *The Complete Juggler*, and fulfill all of your juggling ambitions.

As you progress in juggling you will find that there is great depth to this apparently "trivial" pursuit. Many people experience changes in awareness and energy which they did not anticipate. We explore these changes together in *The Zen of Juggling*, a guide book for those who see juggling as a path to personal growth.

You may want to supplement these books with videos, and we have two series for you. *Juggling Step by Step* is a two hour video version of *The Complete Juggler*, with hundreds of tricks presented in slow and fast motion by experts. Most recently we have produced a series of thirty minute musical instructional children's videos that use original songs to teach juggling. The basic three tape series works from age 5 up. It includes *JUGGLETIME*™, which comes with a set of nylon scarves, *JUGGLING STAR*™ covering balls and beanbags, and *JUGGLERS' JAM*™ covering rings, clubs and everything else. We have even produced the definitive juggling exercise tape, *JUGGLERCISE*™, presenting a dozen songs for scarf juggling fun. These tapes are entertaining as well as instructional.

We have dedicated the past fifteen years to creating high quality juggling "props" at reasonable prices for beginning, intermediate and advanced jugglers. There are now more than seventy separate items in the JUGGLEBUG™ inventory. Check at the store where you bought this book for our products. If you can't find them there, call any magic store and ask if they carry the JUGGLEBUG™ line of juggling products. If there is no magic store nearby, try a high quality toy store, kite shop, costume or theatrical supply shop or alternative sporting goods store. If you cannot find JUGGLEBUG™ products nearby, please check the appendix for sources, or give us a call at (206) 774-2127 and we'll either help you locate a source or send you a retail catalog.

Finally, and most important, you will soon find out that juggling is a wonderful pastime. Don't keep it to yourself. Once you know how to juggle, pass the skill around. Teach others, and move on beyond solo juggling to passing with a partner. Get together with other jugglers, share the skills you have just learned and work on new moves.

Remember, a drop is a sign of progress, and everyone learns to juggle drop by drop.

Dave Finnigan
Edmonds, WA

JUGGLING AND YOU

Juggling is a series of challenges. The first challenge is simply to throw one object from hand to hand following a specific pattern. Once you can throw one, you can exchange two; and after you can exchange two, you can juggle three. If you have three objects under control you can begin to play with the infinite variations found in this book and in your imagination.

Jugglebug is dedicated to introducing as many people as possible to the joy of juggling. Almost anyone can juggle. It is not an art form reserved for circus people, but is a physically and mentally relaxing form of recreation which can help you to discover and to nurture your innate coordination. Once you have learned how, juggling, like swimming, is impossible to forget. So it is a skill that you can keep for life. Unlike most sports, juggling is completely portable and you can do it almost anywhere either alone, with a partner, or in a group.

Another characteristic of juggling is its rhythmic, almost musical nature. It can have the same calming effect on your spirit as playing or listening to good music. For many, juggling is a form of meditation, of integrating mind, body, and spirit.

Juggling is an infinite art form. The patterns you can weave in the air with 2, 3, 4, 5, or more balls, rings or clubs or with 2, 3, 4, 5, or more people are beyond reckoning. Each time you learn a trick you see or think up a new one; and you are continually extending the upper limit (or "leading edge") of your capability. After a month or a year or a decade of juggling one thing stands out—how far ahead you are compared to where you were when you started or where you ever thought you could be. What looked impossible just a while ago is now a part of your routine and now something far more difficult appears impossible. The horizon retreats endlessly before you. Jugglers are very supportive of one another. Each person is at a level determined by his or her ability and by the amount of time and energy given over to juggling. Unlike other activities, in juggling you can plan for and experience your own growth. Once you have conquered the basic "cascade" pattern you will also be able to overcome any nervousness about juggling in front of others. Dropping the balls is not a sign of clumsiness, it is a sign of progress, showing that there is growth going on.

At Jugglebug we suggest you carry your equipment with you at all times, in your executive brief case or your junior executive backpack. Your bumper sticker or any of the achievement pins will identify you as a juggler. When you meet a fellow juggler don't hesitate, get out your equipment and share information. Let's fill the hallways of office buildings, parks and freeway rest stops with jugglers.

Some sports seem to foster impatience, a sense of frustration and the sort of destructive competition which makes half the participants in any event into losers. You will find that juggling can help you to develop patience, self-confidence, and an ability to work smoothly with others. There are no losers, and you only compete with yourself.

Most of all juggling is joyous. It is a release of energy in the form of creativity which gives instant, personal, internal rewards to the participant (aside from any applause or from the bills which may mysteriously appear in one's up-turned cap following a particularly self-satisfying routine).

If you use the Jugglebug method, by the time you go to bed tonight you should be able to report with glee, "Look, Ma—I'm Jugglin'." Within a month you should be able to put on a show which actually draws applause, "oohs" and "ahs." Before we begin this adventure, let's toss a few basic points up into the air.

First — If at any time you feel tight, frustrated or klutzy, or if you find yourself repeating the same mistakes over and over, stop at the exact moment of your error. Then close your eyes and think through what you were trying to do. Figure out what went wrong. Try to see it right in your mind's eye. Figure out what you have to do to correct the error, shake your arms and shoulders to loosen up; then reopen your eyes and begin again. Like a springboard diver, the juggler must make all of his or her conscious decisions before going into the air. Unlike diving, the performer remains dry and the balls take the belly flops.

Second — There is a logical progression to this book in general, and to each chapter. Rather than jumping around, proceed page by page from the front to the back of each chapter. Don't move on to the next step until you have full control over what comes before it. This way you can avoid developing or reinforcing bad habits. If you start to get sloppy, go back and perfect the previous step before moving forward again.

Third — Keep your senses fully engaged in what you are doing, but don't depend much on your conscious mind and on the thinking process once the balls start to fly. Thinking takes too much time. Try to feel the pattern that the balls should be making with your body and with your senses. Concentrate the thinking part of your mind on the leading edge, the point at which you made your last error. If step 4 is where you are goofing up, let steps 1, 2 and 3 flow automatically while you concentrate on the movements required in step 4. If you can't do this, you shouldn't be on step 4 yet and should go back and reexperience steps 1 through 3 until they don't tie up your conscious mind.

Fourth — While learning, imagine that you are in a phone booth with a ceiling just a foot over the top of your head. The glass walls and ceiling of this booth are very fragile. Don't let your balls hit the walls or ceiling or the whole building will shatter. Your act takes place entirely within the phone booth until you have gained sufficient control to make longer throws at will. Don't let your friends talk you into testing how high or how far out to the side you can throw until you can juggle in a phone booth.

Carlo, author of "The Juggling Book", uses the term "wall plane" to describe the path the balls should follow. The wall plane is an imaginary surface about a foot in front of you. The balls stay generally in this plane, exept when you consciously try to make them deviate from it. Carlo uses the term "tray plane" to describe the "home" position of your hands. This is the plane formed by your hands held palm up, as if you were carrying a tray. These ideas may be useful for your own practice and will be used occasionally in the book.

Fifth — You will be tempted to rely on your dominant hand, your right if you are right handed, your left if you are left handed. Give your subordinate hand a workout whenever possible. As soon as you have learned a trick with your dominant hand, switch and learn it with the subordinate hand taking the lead. You will find that any effort with your subordinate hand will transfer easily to the dominant hand whereas the reverse is not necessarily true.

Sixth — Finish cleanly. You will shortly learn how to start and stop a juggling routine. The clean finish is essential to learn and to practice. Don't just juggle until the act falls apart. Choose a number of repetitions at which to stop and cut off sharply.

Seventh — Juggle with a friend whenever possible. Use the buddy system to check up on each other's progress. Anyone who uses this book can be a teacher. Help one another to avoid bad habits. For example, if your partner throws too far forward, stand in front of him and act as a living wall. Caution him not to hit you upon pain of punching. You will be surprised how quickly he will get those throws under control!

Eighth — Keep a record of your progress. We provide a form for that purpose in the back of the book. Set a goal for every practice session and set overall goals. Practice is the only key to perfection.

Enough Talk — Now on to the action!

SCARF JUGGLING

* Note: To get equipment look in Appendix I for juggling resources and addresses

THE CASCADE

STEP 1—THROWING 1 SCARF

Hold one scarf in the center like a ghost.

Lift your arm as high as you can across your chest.

Toss the scarf with your palm out, like waving goodbye.

Reach high up with your other hand and catch straight down.

Claw like a lion.

Now raise that arm across in the other direction

6

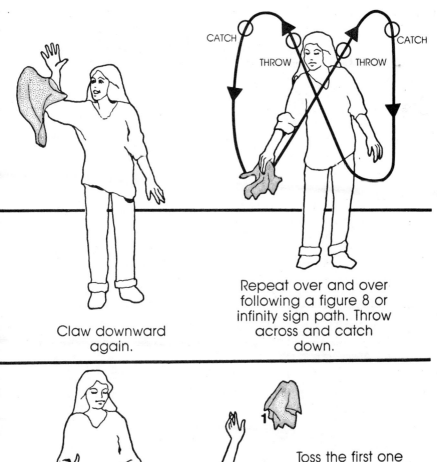

CATCH · THROW · THROW · CATCH

Claw downward again.

Repeat over and over following a figure 8 or infinity sign path. Throw across and catch down.

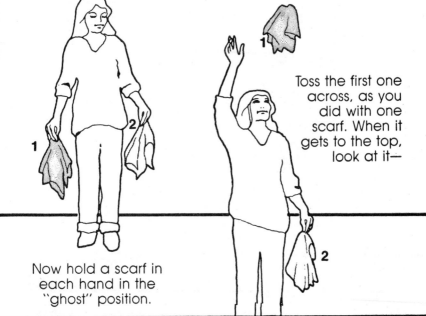

Now hold a scarf in each hand in the "ghost" position.

Toss the first one across, as you did with one scarf. When it gets to the top, look at it—

And throw the second scarf across in the opposite direction. The scarves make an "X" across your chest.

Catch the first scarf straight down, then catch the second one. Throw-Throw-Catch-Catch.

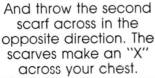

MOVING RIGHT ALONG.

THREE SCARVES!

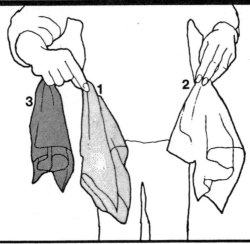

Now hold one scarf on your fingertips in the hand that has two. That's the first scarf you throw.

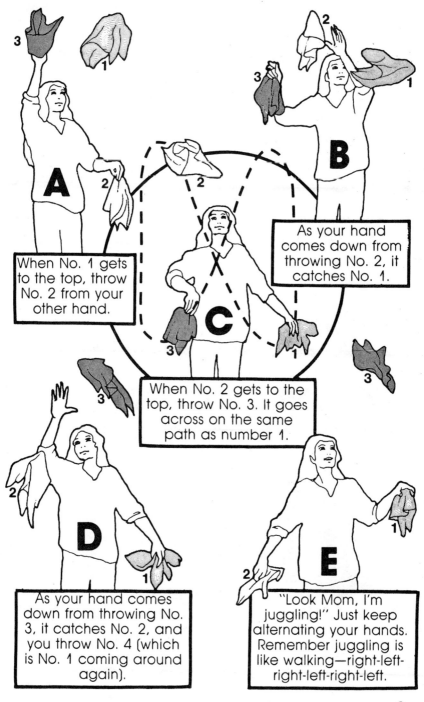

A

When No. 1 gets to the top, throw No. 2 from your other hand.

B

As your hand comes down from throwing No. 2, it catches No. 1.

C

When No. 2 gets to the top, throw No. 3. It goes across on the same path as number 1.

D

As your hand comes down from throwing No. 3, it catches No. 2, and you throw No. 4 (which is No. 1 coming around again).

E

"Look Mom, I'm juggling!" Just keep alternating your hands. Remember juggling is like walking—right-left-right-left-right-left.

9

Accelerated Learning

• Juggling is rhythmic, so why not turn on the music. In fact, you will learn faster if you put on a record with a good solid beat.

• Take a challenge. If you did three good throws, go on to four, if you did four, go on to ten, go for 20 or 50. Count your throws and keep exceeding your old record.

• Don't be satisfied just knowing this one pattern. Learn all the moves in this chapter, and then invent some new ones.

NOW THAT YOU'VE GOTTEN STARTED, HERE'S HOW TO KEEP GOING....

1. START WITH THE HAND THAT HAS 2 SCARVES IN IT.
2. THROW ACROSS YOUR BODY WITH AN "X", RELEASING AS HIGH AS POSSIBLE.
3. LOOK AT THE TOP.
4. EVERY TIME ONE GETS TO THE TOP, THROW ANOTHER, THEN CATCH THE ONE THAT'S IN THE AIR
5. ALTERNATE YOUR HANDS AND COUNT "1-2-1-2", OR "LEFT-RIGHT-LEFT."
6. TAKE YOUR TIME, SCARF JUGGLING IS SOFT AND FLOWING.
7. DROPPING IS A SIGN OF PROGRESS
8. HAVE FUN AND TEACH OTHERS!

NOTE: The basic cascade is often perceived as three objects thrown in the air simultaneously. In fact, most of the time there is one object in the air, sometimes two, but never three.

REVERSE CASCADE

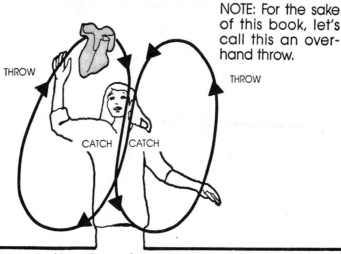

THROW

THROW

NOTE: For the sake of this book, let's call this an over- hand throw.

CATCH CATCH

Throw one scarf in a figure 8, but this time it is a throw which goes over the top from the outside of the pattern, and straight down the center.

1

2

Start with one in each hand. Throw one scarf overhand. When it begins to come down the center, throw the second with a big overhand movement. Catch the first, catch the second.

11

NOW TRY 3 SCARVES. Just imagine you have a bucket in front of you at eye level, start with the hand that has two, and toss them in the bucket, one by one.
1
2
3

COLUMNS– THE EASIEST MOVE.

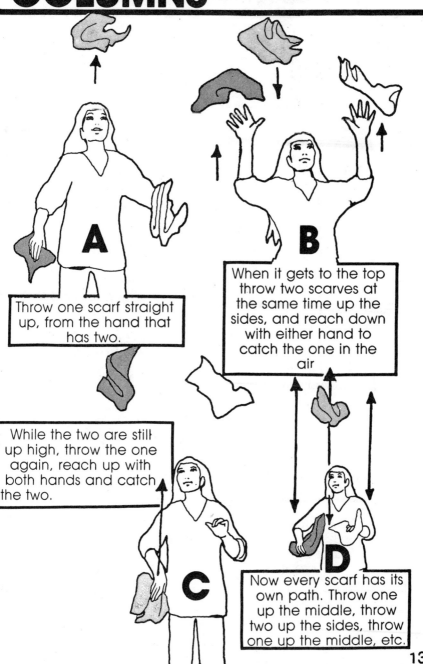

A
Throw one scarf straight up, from the hand that has two.

B
When it gets to the top throw two scarves at the same time up the sides, and reach down with either hand to catch the one in the air

C
While the two are still up high, throw the one again, reach up with both hands and catch the two.

D
Now every scarf has its own path. Throw one up the middle, throw two up the sides, throw one up the middle, etc.

13

SIDE BY SIDE

Stand side by side. One person takes two scarves, the other takes one. The person with two starts.

Now you are just a 2 headed, two handed, four legged juggling creature.

BALL JUGGLING

THE CASCADE

The first juggling move is called the "Cascade."
It's as basic and simple as walking, and is a rest
position to which the juggler can return at will.
Like any new skill, juggling moves are best learned
step by step, and the keys are consistency and
repetition. Never be afraid to make the next throw,
just keep trying until you get it right.

STEP 1 ONE BALL

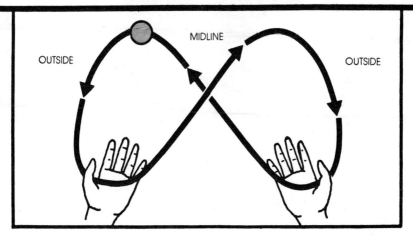

Start with one ball. Throw it from hand to hand in a "Figure
8" or infinity sign pattern, with scooping underhand throws.
Let go of the ball toward the midline of your body, and
catch it toward the outside, carrying it back to the midline
to throw again.

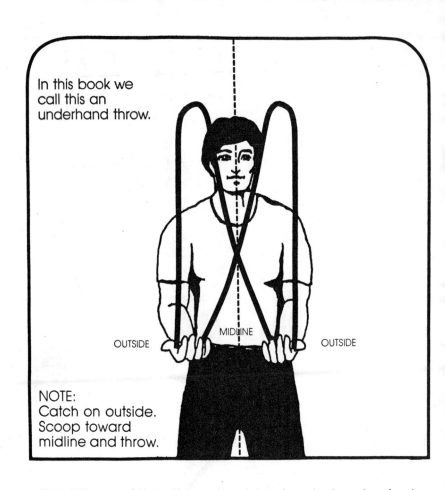

In this book we call this an underhand throw.

OUTSIDE

MIDLINE

OUTSIDE

NOTE:
Catch on outside.
Scoop toward
midline and throw.

This "Figure 8" pattern should extend about a foot above your shoulder on each side. Keep your hands down. Don't reach up higher than your chest to throw or catch. Keep the ball on a plane in front of you.

When you can make a smooth figure 8 without pauses, and without recoiling or cocking your hand before throwing, you have passed the juggler's test. Repeat ten times and move on to Step 2.

STEP 2 **STARTING AND STOPPING**

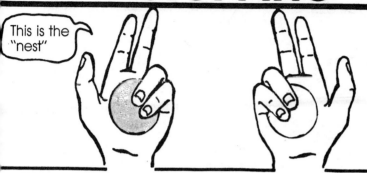

This is the "nest"

Pick up two balls and hold them on the heels of your hands as shown so that you have room in the nest formed by your thumb, forefinger and middle finger for a third ball.

SCOOP   SCOOP

Pick up a third ball and throw it from hand to hand, from nest to nest, following the path described in Step 1.

Remember the figure 8. You are not juggling yet. This is just a warm-up exercise to teach you how to begin and end the juggling routine.

When you can throw one ball from nest to nest ten times in a row without dropping it, move on Step 3.

EXCHANGING TWO BALLS

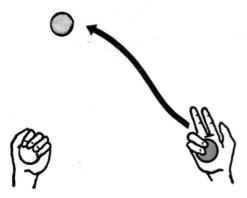

Hold two balls in your dominant hand and one in your subordinate hand. Throw the ball from the nest of your dominant hand, and say "one" in a loud voice. Follow the figure 8 path.

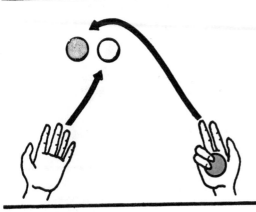

When the ball peaks, say "two" and throw the ball out of your subordinate hand, scooping it underneath the first ball as shown, also following the figure 8 path.

The two balls should cross in the air and change hands.

When you can exchange two balls ten times in a row without a drop, move on to Step 4.

CONTINUING TO JUGGLE

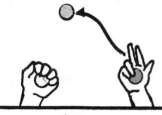

Start again. Throw the first ball from your dominant hand, just as you did in the previous step and say "one."

When Ball 1 peaks, throw the ball from your subordinate hand and say "two."

When Ball 2 peaks, throw the ball from your dominant hand and say "three."

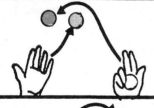

When Ball 3 peaks, throw the ball from your subordinate hand and say "four."

When Ball 4 peaks, throw the ball from your dominant hand and say "five."

Keep throwing and keep counting.

NOTE: Learn to start with two balls in your subordinate hand. You should be able to start with either hand and finish in either hand.

REMEMBER

1. Start with the hand that has two.
2. Every time a ball peaks, throw another one with a scooping underhand throw.
3. Alternate hands left-right-left-right-left-right.
4. Throw to the same height on both sides.
5. Focus on the peaks. Don't look at your hands.
6. Count out loud, or say "right-left-right-left."
7. When you want to stop, stop cleanly by catching the last ball on your three finger nest.
8. Remember every ball follows that same figure 8 path.
9. Keep the balls in a plane in front of you —don't throw them forward.
10. There should always be one ball in the air, and one on the way up.
11. Go slowly, wait for those peaks, don't worry about drops—a dropped ball is a sign of progress.
12. Eventually give up the counting, and bring the whole pattern down below your eyes. That's where more controlled juggling begins.

Now that you have this basic "Cascade" pattern, you have taken the most difficult step in juggling. Don't be complacent; move on to additional tricks.

REVERSE CASCADE

In the Cascade, you throw underhand, from near the midline, and catch on the outside. In the reverse Cascade, you throw from the outside, and catch near the midline, still following a figure 8 path.

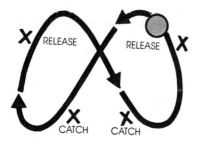

Start by throwing one ball overhand. Release the ball at shoulder height, catch it with your opposite hand at waist height.

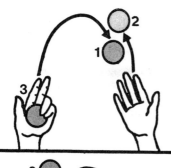

As soon as you can throw one ball hand to hand, try two. Hold one in each hand. Throw the first one. When it peaks, throw the second up over it. The balls cross in the air and change hands.

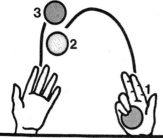

Now just keep going. Every time a ball peaks, throw another one over it, following the same path. Focus on the peaks.

CLAWING

Clawing means bringing your hand down over the descending ball and throwing backhanded. To learn to claw, start with one ball. Toss it backhanded from hand to hand, bringing your forearm and hand down to meet the ball, palm downward, when it has descended about halfway from the peak of its path to your waist.

Turn your wrist slightly to the inside and throw it back with your palm out. Your throwing hand reaches across your body with your palm out, like waving goodbye.

Once you can toss one ball back and forth fairly uniformly, move right up to three balls.

As you work on this part of the routine, it is vital that you keep your arms and hands down as much as possible and keep the ball in toward your body; don't let it fly away. You will probably find that this is a very rhythmic movement which certainly accentuates the outside catch and the inside throw.

Well, if you've gotten this far, you are starting to feel the effects of juggling. This ancient art is a fine spiritual, mental and physical journey. Keep on juggling. Don't quit now. There are still lots more tricks to learn.

TWO BALLS
IN ONE HAND

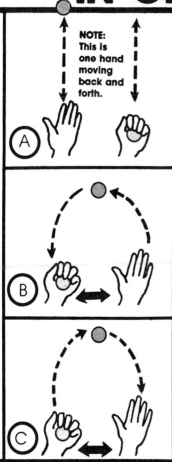

NOTE:
This is
one hand
moving
back and
forth.

The timing for this move is the same as for three ball juggling. Every time a ball reaches the peak, you throw the other one; so just focus on the peaks.

You can throw each ball in its own column (A), in a circle toward the outside (B) or in a circle toward the inside (C).

It is important in this move to keep the balls in a plane in front of your body. Work in height and width, not depth. Don't shovel in towards yourself, just go from side to side.

THE SHOWER

In many parts of the world, this move is all there is to juggling. One hand does all the throwing, the other does all the catching, and the balls move in a circle over the juggler's head.

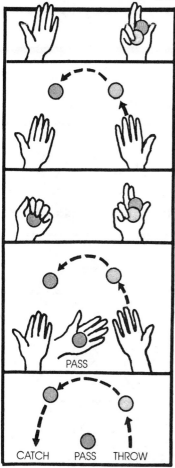

PASS

CATCH   PASS   THROW

Start with two balls in your dominant hand. Throw them one at a time in a high arc so rapidly that the second ball is well on its way when the first lands. Repeat ten times.

Put one ball in your subordinate hand. Throw the two from your dominant in rapid succession, and just before the first ball lands, pass the third ball across and throw it with your dominant hand.

Then every time a ball lands in your subordinate hand, immediately pass it across and throw it in that same high arc from the dominant hand.

Accuracy and speed are the keys to a successful shower. Just keep throwing as fast as possible and keep catching with your subordinate hand and passing across.

JUGGLERS' TENNIS

Now that you can juggle with underhand throws (cascade) and overhand throws (reverse cascade), you can combine the two.

Toss over with the right and under with the left, or

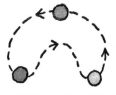

Toss under with the right and over with the left.

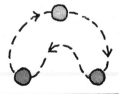

Now juggle with three balls, one of which is distinctly different. The trick is to juggle a cascade with the other two (number 1 and number 2), but to toss that "odd" ball (number 3) back and forth over the top. You can shoot lobs or smashes with this tennis ball.

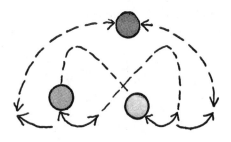

Number 1 and number 2 are the net; number 3 is the tennis ball.

Some Practice Points

- Remember to set a goal for each practice session.
- Stretch and limber up before practicing.
- Pay attention to your posture. Keep your back straight and chest out.
- Juggle over mats or sand if available to minimize wear and tear on equipment.
- Practice to non-obtrusive music with a solid beat.
- Whenever you start a practice session go through a routine of the tricks you already know. Then work on something new until you get it.
- If possible, occasionally videotape a practice session. Whenever possible, practice in front of a mirror.
- Keep these slogans in mind:
  "A drop is a sign of progress."
  "A touch is as good as a catch—because you knew where it was headed."
  "End every practice session with an accomplishment."
  "Anything is possible with a good plan, practice and commitment."

THE YO-YO (AND THE OY-OY)

Once you can juggle two in one hand a series of entertaining tricks is possible.

1. Juggle 2 balls in columns in your dominant hand, each one in its own pathway. Hold your other hand out where you can see it, but don't move it yet, just get used to seeing it there.

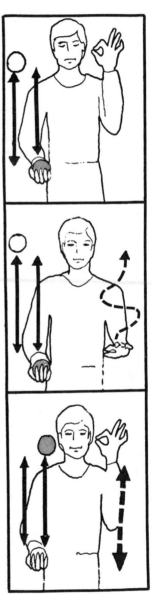

2. Now begin to move that other hand around. Start with random movements.

3. Now keep one of the balls you are juggling in mind. Every time you throw it, raise your other hand. Parallel the movement of this one ball with your empty hand.

4. Now do this same step, but hold a ball in the subordinate hand. (You could call this move the "bar-bell" since the two balls appear to be connected by an invisible rod.)

5. Now move the subordinate hand up and down above that one ball. Keep the same distance between the ball in your subordinate hand and the one you seem to be pulling up and pushing down with an invisible string.

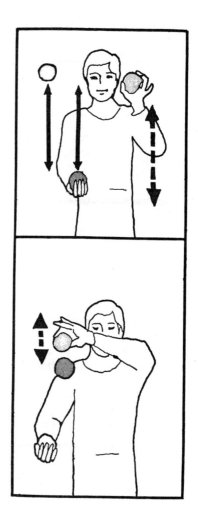

Although these variations of one handed juggling are relatively simple, people don't know it; and kids especially will giggle and "ooh" and "ah" at this part of your routine.

COLUMNS

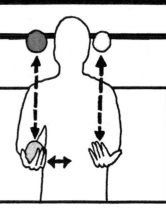

Start with two balls in your dominant hand and one in the subordinate. Start by throwing a ball from each hand simultaneously.

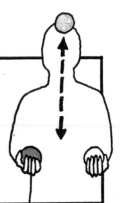

When the two balls peak, throw the third up the Center. Catch the two and throw them again. Now every time the one peaks, throw two and every time the two peak throw one.

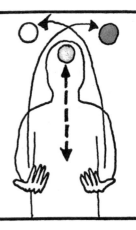

For variety, when you throw the two balls arc them in toward the center so they cross in the air and change hands. If you keep one hand forward and one hand back a bit, the two balls won't hit. Or else you can throw one high and one low every time.

Now that you can throw straight up and down and cross the balls at will, try a few variations.

Toss two balls as if to cross them, but throw them with equal and identical force. They will bump into one another and fall back into their respective throwing hands.

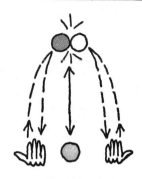

Toss two balls straight up and throw the third ball back and forth over the top of the two. This is a variation of jugglers' tennis.

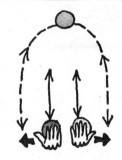

A simpler method of kissing is a planned collision on the way up. Use two balls to practice, throw them in toward one another and slightly upward.

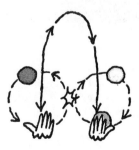

THE SEE SAW

Start with 2 balls in the right hand and 1 in the left.

① ③   ②

Toss the ball on the fingertips of the right hand straight up.

① ↑ ③   ②

When it peaks toss the solo ball in the left hand straight up, and

① ③   ② ↑

Toss the third ball straight across from right to left.

↓ ①——→③   ②

When the first ball lands, toss it straight up again and immediately

① ↑   ② ↓ ③

Toss the third ball back across from left to right as the second ball lands.

①
③←——②

Now number 1 and number 2 go straight up and down, and number 3 goes back and forth from hand to hand.

BODY SHOTS

You can throw an occasional ball or a series of balls under or behind some part of your body. Some of the most common of these moves are:

UNDER THE LEG

To learn easily, raise your knee and throw your first ball under that leg to start juggling.

Raise your knee

Toss the first ball under to start

Now you can go under your leg in the middle of the juggling pattern. As soon as you have thrown with your right hand, raise your knee and toss the next right hand throw under your knee. Lower your leg and keep juggling.

BEHIND THE BACK

Practice with one ball. Toss it from your right hand behind your back across and up over your left shoulder. Catch it in front in the left hand. Then toss it behind your back across and up over your right shoulder and catch it in yor right hand.

Toss behind back with right hand.

Catch in front with left hand.

Toss behind back with left hand.

Catch in front with right hand.

Now move on to two balls.

With one ball in each hand, toss behind the back with the right, and as that ball comes into view over your left shoulder, toss the ball from your left hand across to the right in a normal cascade.

Toss with right hand behind back and over left shoulder...

Look to left and as the ball comes into view...

Throw the one in your left hand up and across.

Now try the same move while juggling. Concentrate on one ball. When that ball comes to your right hand reach behind your back and throw up and across your back so it comes over your left shoulder.

While juggling, reach back and throw with the right hand.

Now reach out and catch the ball that is coming toward your right hand. Pause.

As the ball comes into view throw from the left and continue.

Once you can throw over either shoulder consistently you can throw over both shoulders sequentially. This is a BACKCROSS.

Toss with the right, look to the left.

Toss with the left, look to the right.

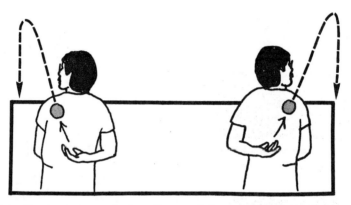

Now that you can do two throws in succession, try three balls and three throws. Then do four throws, five, six and seven. Work your way up, one throw at a time, until you can just keep going.

POINTERS:
- Reach high to throw and practice with one ball and two balls until smooth and precise.
- Practice turning your head from side to side, moving your arms but not throwing.
- Throw higher than usual to give yourself more time.
- Your catches are all in front and are blind since your head is turned the opposite way when you catch.
- Your throws are all from the back and must be precise to make catching easier.

OVER THE SHOULDER

Learn this move one ball at a time as you did with the previous one. The only differences are:

1. The ball comes over the shoulder of the hand that threw it;
2. The next throw is from that same hand.

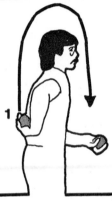

Toss up and over the same shoulder. (This will feel like a contortion at first.)

When the ball comes into view toss the next throw from that same hand. Keep juggling.

Of course you can go in the opposite direction. Toss over the shoulder toward the back. The next throw is across the chest with the same hand; then reach back and catch. Bring that hand back to the front. Resume juggling.

BOUNCING ON THE FLOOR

Learn to bounce just as you learned the cascade. Bounce one ball back and forth in front of you. Once you can do this successfully, throw one ball down, as soon as it hits the ground, throw the second ball so that it goes outside of the first, hits the same spot, and bounces to the other hand. Now try three.

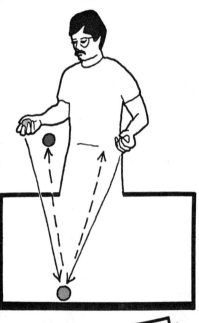

Now work on putting your leg through the bouncing pattern so one ball goes under your leg.

Note: Learn this on both sides, then quickly alternate your legs and bounce under alternately from both sides.

1—Throw down;
2—Raise your knee;
3—The ball bounces under your leg;
4—Straighten your leg.

While juggling, toss one ball extra high and let it bounce. Pause. When it comes back up past your hands, imagine it is the first ball in a cascade pattern, and start juggling.

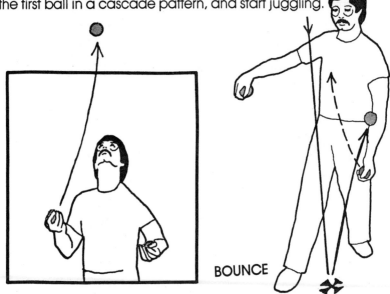

BOUNCE

Now try the same move with two extra-high throws and two bounces. Remember which ball you threw first. When it peaks, throw number 3 under it. Catch and throw number 1, catch and throw number 2, catch and throw number 3.

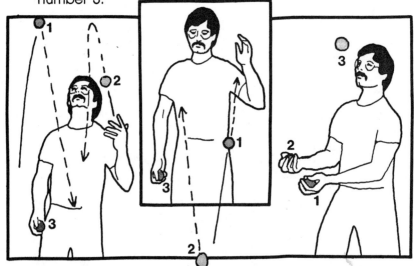

Now you can throw and catch all three balls in turn. Just remember the colors of the balls. If you throw red, yellow, blue, catch red, yellow, blue, and start juggling again. Just throw, throw, throw, bounce, bounce, bounce, catch, catch, toss and catch.

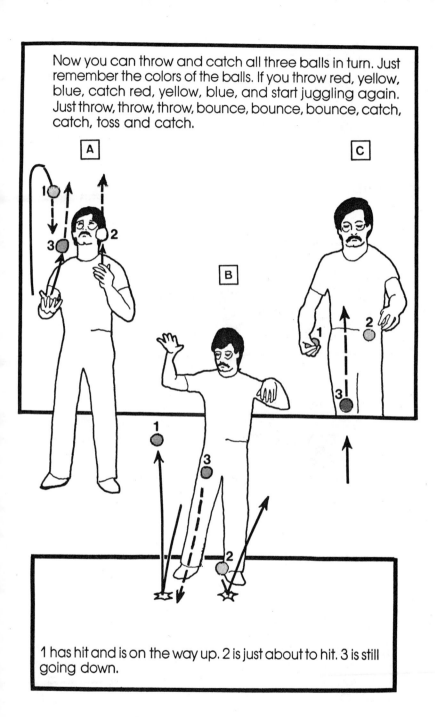

1 has hit and is on the way up. 2 is just about to hit. 3 is still going down.

Toss all 3 balls into the air in a triangle, keeping them separated and at the same height.

Let them fall onto a bouncy wooden floor.

When they come back up, claw downward on the outer two before they peak. The center ball bounces up high and you start juggling as if it were the first ball in a cascade.

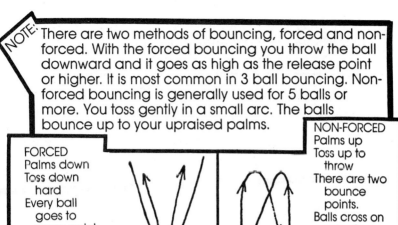

NOTE: There are two methods of bouncing, forced and non-forced. With the forced bouncing you throw the ball downward and it goes as high as the release point or higher. It is most common in 3 ball bouncing. Non-forced bouncing is generally used for 5 balls or more. You toss gently in a small arc. The balls bounce up to your upraised palms.

FORCED
Palms down
Toss down
 hard
Every ball
 goes to
 same point
Balls go down
 the outside
They come up
 the inside

NON-FORCED
Palms up
Toss up to
 throw
There are two
 bounce
 points.
Balls cross on
 way down
Balls go down
 the inside
Balls come up
 the outside

"ENGLISH"

Usually the angle at which the ball goes down is about the same as the angle at which it comes up. For a special bouncing effort you can put "English" (forward spin or back spin) on the ball. This makes the ball bounce erratically. With English you can toss the ball away and make it bounce back to you.

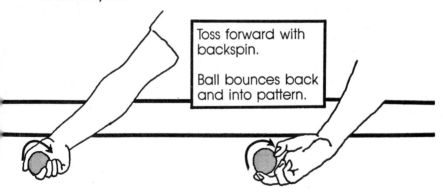

Toss forward with backspin.

Ball bounces back and into pattern.

To put backspin on the ball, as you throw it pull down with your thumb over the top.

To put forward spin on the ball, simply pull your hand out from under and rotate the ball as you throw.

pull this way
ball spins inward

Toss over your
shoulder with
forward spin.

Ball bounces
behind your back
and up into pattern.

BODY BOUNCES

Just think of all the parts of your body where a ball or beanbag can be bounced. Toss one ball to that spot, bounce it and catch it. Then toss one, bounce it off and start juggling. Finally, toss out of the juggle, bounce, and keep going.

You can bounce off your

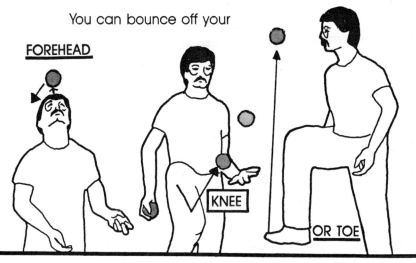

FOREHEAD

KNEE

OR TOE

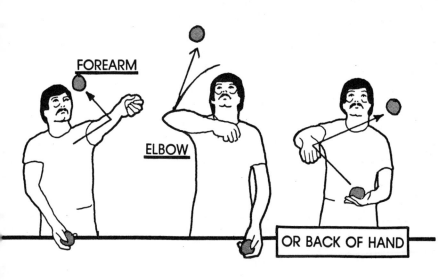

FOREARM

ELBOW

OR BACK OF HAND

If you spend some time in practice you can bounce a ball repeatedly from...

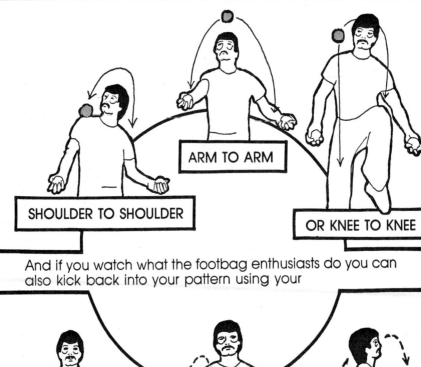

ARM TO ARM

SHOULDER TO SHOULDER

OR KNEE TO KNEE

And if you watch what the footbag enthusiasts do you can also kick back into your pattern using your

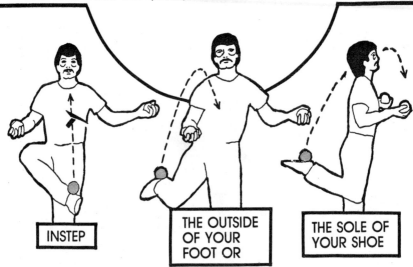

INSTEP

THE OUTSIDE OF YOUR FOOT OR

THE SOLE OF YOUR SHOE

The key in all of this is to practice smaller and smaller bounces and lighter and lighter taps. Finesse is more important than force.

FLASHY STARTS

For a simple flashy start toss both the balls from your right hand into the air with an outward twist of your wrist. The balls split as shown.

Now toss the third ball up through the split. Catch the two, one in each hand.

When the two come down toss one immediately across to the other hand and begin a cascade.

Even fancier is to hold all three balls in your dominant hand (Step 1).

1

Toss all three at once. The center ball goes higher than the other two (Step 2).

2

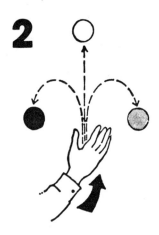

When the two outer balls are at their peaks, reach up and claw down on them (Step 3) while the center ball continues to climb.

3

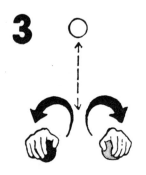

As the center ball starts to fall, toss the right hand ball up and across in a cascade pattern (Step 4). Now you are juggling.

4

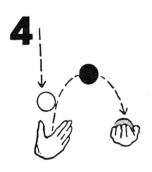

THE KICK BACK

When juggling bouncy balls you can retrieve a drop by stepping hard on the ball as it bounces away, pulling your foot in toward you at the same time. The errant ball will bounce up and back, high enough to work it into your routine. As it comes to you, toss the ball from the hand that is about to receive the runaway ball, and begin your routine again.

If you lose a ball and it goes so far away that you can't retrieve it, you can still salvage the act. As soon as an audience member touches it point straight at them and exclaim, "My first volunteer." Direct them to lob the ball to you. As it comes in resume juggling.

Whatever you do, never act flustered if you drop. It's part of the act. Keep going!

RECOVERIES

Turn your drops into applause points.

Clasp the dropped beanbag between your heels—

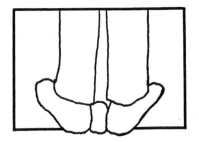

Kick up and bring your feet to one side, so the beanbag goes over one shoulder—

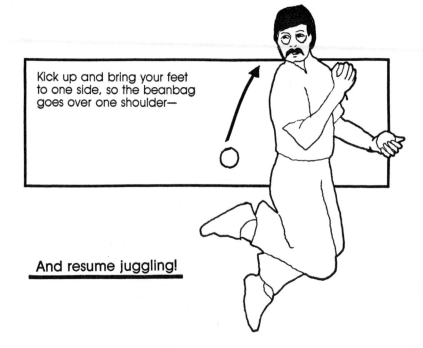

And resume juggling!

Or roll the beanbag onto your toe with your other foot and kick it up, into the pattern.

Or drop the other two beanbags and make a "shell game" out of it by hopping the beanbags over one another on the ground, in a cascade pattern.

THREE BALL INTERACTION

Once you can juggle three balls or beanbags it is time to find or develop a partner. Working together takes patience, but develops it as well. Remember to laugh occasionally, and **never** blame yourself or your partner for drops. Nobody's perfect.

THE TAKE-AWAY

Face your partner and get close, so you could share a juggling space. Your partner starts juggling slowly with three balls, one of which is a different color. Just watch that different colored ball, and when your partner throws it from her right to her left reach up with your right hand and take it at the moment when it peaks.

This ball came from your partner's right hand.

Get a nice high pattern to start.

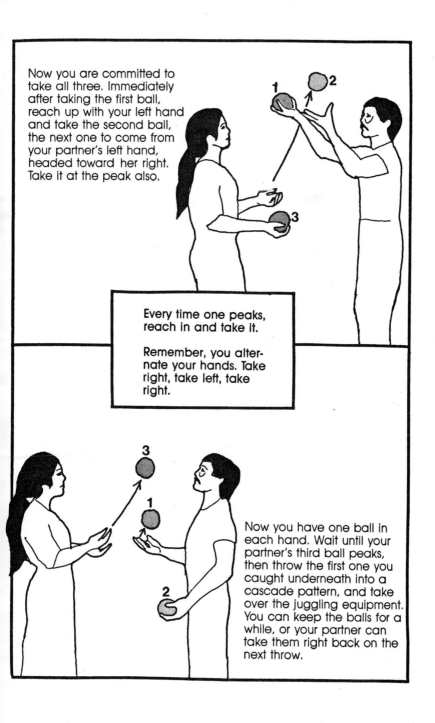

Now you are committed to take all three. Immediately after taking the first ball, reach up with your left hand and take the second ball, the next one to come from your partner's left hand, headed toward her right. Take it at the peak also.

Every time one peaks, reach in and take it.

Remember, you alternate your hands. Take right, take left, take right.

Now you have one ball in each hand. Wait until your partner's third ball peaks, then throw the first one you caught underneath into a cascade pattern, and take over the juggling equipment. You can keep the balls for a while, or your partner can take them right back on the next throw.

Now that you can take three balls from the front you can grab them with your palms up, with your palms down (clawing), and by chopping into the balls from the inside or outside.

Once you feel comfortable taking all 3 balls, just take out one, and replace it in the pattern. Your partner keeps juggling the remaining 2 balls at a normal cadence, with an empty space for the missing ball. As soon as possible find this space, and toss or drop the stolen ball back into the pattern.

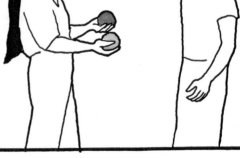

RUNNING THREE

This is a lead-in to passing six objects and is a great way to practice passing tricks without having to worry about drops.

Start juggling three balls, facing your partner, about 6 feet apart. After you are stabilized, toss one of your right-hand throws across to your partner's left.

Now every right-hand throw goes across to your partner's left. All your left-hand throws go across your chest from left to right in the usual pattern. Remember to alternate your throws as usual.

Your partner catches the incoming balls in the left-hand one by one, and throws across her chest to her right in the usual manner.

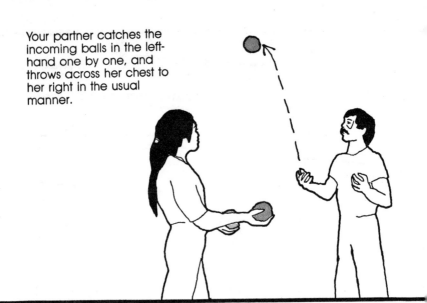

As soon as she is stabilized she can throw across to you again from her right.

The balls make a rectangle, from your left, to your right, to her left, to her right, and back to your left. Remember to alternate your hands and to throw across your chest with your left hand.

PASSING 5, 6, 7 AND MORE BALLS

Now that you can share three balls with a partner, you are beginning to appreciate the joy of interactive juggling. You can probably see how learning to pass six balls will lead inevitably to passing six or more clubs. In terms of audience appeal, working with a partner is usually far more impressive than a solo routine.

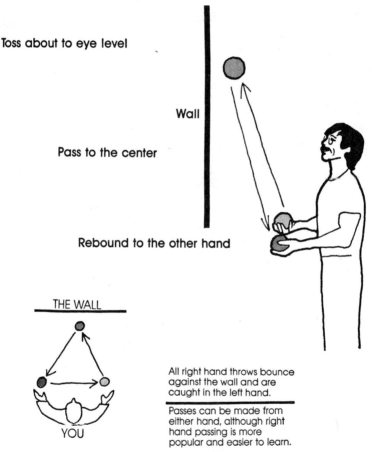

Toss about to eye level

Wall

Pass to the center

Rebound to the other hand

THE WALL

YOU

All right hand throws bounce against the wall and are caught in the left hand.

Passes can be made from either hand, although right hand passing is more popular and easier to learn.

You can begin to learn ball passing by bouncing against a wall. Although the motion of throwing to a wall is diagonal rather than straight across as in real partnership juggling, the wall is a great way to learn when practicing alone.

3-3-10

The most common 6-object passing pattern is one called "3-3-10" in which every third ball leaving your right hand is passed across to your partner three times; everysecond right hand ball is then passed three times; and finally every right hand ball is passed 10 times, in a flurry of activity.

←   6 ft.   →

To begin any passing routine, stand facing your partner about six feet away. Hold the balls just as you did for the beginning of the basic cascade, except that both of you start as if you were right handed. In other words, put two balls in the right hand and one in the left hand.

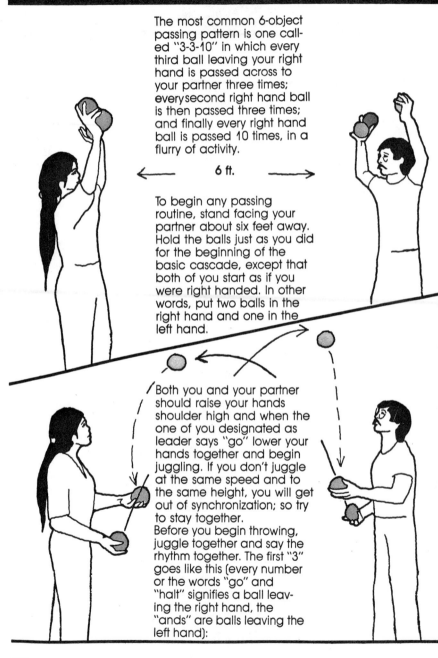

Both you and your partner should raise your hands shoulder high and when the one of you designated as leader says "go" lower your hands together and begin juggling. If you don't juggle at the same speed and to the same height, you will get out of synchronization; so try to stay together.

Before you begin throwing, juggle together and say the rhythm together. The first "3" goes like this (every number or the words "go" and "halt" signifies a ball leaving the right hand, the "ands" are balls leaving the left hand):

"Go, one, and, two, and, throw; and, one, and, two, and, throw; and, one, and, two, and, throw; and, halt."

Now it is best if you and your partner each have an "odd ball." Start with it in your left hand, and your hands held high. Bring them down, and begin.

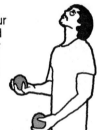

YOUR
THROWS
SHOULD
FOLLOW
A DISTINCT
RECTANGLE

Use the same count, but throw the "odd" ball every time you say "throw" in a clean, eye-high, arc across from your right to your partner's left hand. This throw should be right in with the timing of the rest of the routine, your odd ball goes from your right hand to your partner's left, and his odd ball comes to your left (just as your own odd ball would have if you had thrown it across your own body from right to left, instead of tossing it to your partner).

For this first piece of the routine, your odd balls will be the ones that move. In the next segment every second ball goes across. The count picks up from the third "throw" of the first segment: ". . ., and, one, and, throw; and, one, and, throw; and, one, and, throw; and, halt."

Practice this second segment right after the first, without a break. You may find that your left hand throws are trying to mimic your right hand throws and are going out from your body, causing you to move your right hand and shoulder farther and farther forward. This error can be corrected by practicing alone, close to and facing a wall, and by concentrating on not letting your throws from the left hand (or your right hand itself) touch the wall. Only your right hand throws should go out in front of you, left hand throws should simply cross your body from the left to the right hand.

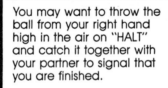

The last throw can go extra high.

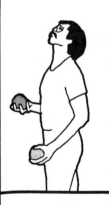

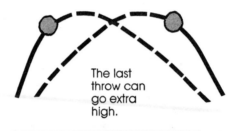

You may want to throw the ball from your right hand high in the air on "HALT" and catch it together with your partner to signal that you are finished.

Now for the third segment. Start off with your sixth "throw" and count: "..., and, throw; and, throw; and, throw; and, throw; and, throw; and, throw; and, throw; and, throw; and, throw; and, throw; and, throw; and, throw; and, HALT."

The full count for "3-3-10" is:
"Go, one, and two, and
throw; and, two, and, two,
and, throw; and three, and,
two, and, throw; and, one,
and throw; and, two, and,
throw; and three, and, throw;
and, throw; and, throw; and,
throw; and, throw; and,
throw; and, throw; and,
throw; and, throw; and,
throw; and, throw; and
HALT."

Catch
that
last
ball
togeth-
er for a
fancy
finish,

In this illustration we have each
switched a ball to our far hand and
caught our final self throw with our
near hand for a fancy finish.

Of course you can try variations of the "3-3-10" routine. However,
you may find that "3-3-3" is about all you can handle at first. The
simplest variation is to have a skinny friend stand in between you
and your partner as you pass, doing a regular cascade pattern.
Or, you can claw every catch, tossing high, hard throws to your
partner. Another, far more difficult, but good for humbling the soul,
is to do all throws with your left hand and catches with your right,
reversing all your habits completely.

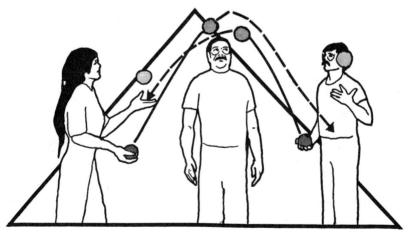

RING JUGGLING
ONE RING

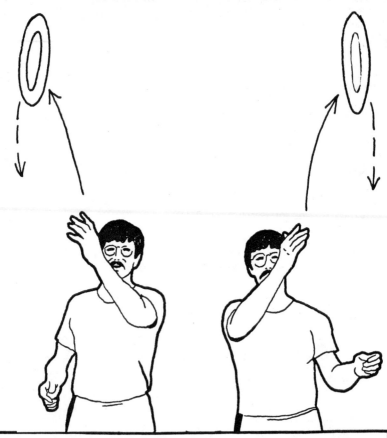

Throw one ring from hand to hand—the sky's the limit—rings can go higher than balls.

★Give the ring a spin as you throw, this will stabilize it.
★You can reach up to throw and catch with rings.
★Tilt your head back and look up.

REMEMBER
THROW NICE AND HIGH WITH TWO PEAKS

TWO RINGS

ONE IN EACH HAND   **READY?**

Throw the first ring. When it reaches its peak, throw the second.

HOLDING THREE RINGS

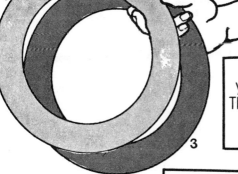

Hold two rings in your dominant hand, The one on your finger tips is the one you throw first.

Hold it loosely. Your second ring is in your other hand.

NOW GO FOR IT! EVERY TIME ONE PEAKS, THROW ANOTHER!

Throw #1;

When #1 gets to the top, throw #2;

When #2 gets to the top, throw #3

COLOR CHANGE

If you have rings with a different color on each side, and want to change the side seen by the audience, there are at least two ways to change it. One is described here, and one in the section on five rings.

While juggling, catch with your palm up and thumb out.

Twist the ring inward and throw again. Keep juggling.

This changes the sides of the ring.

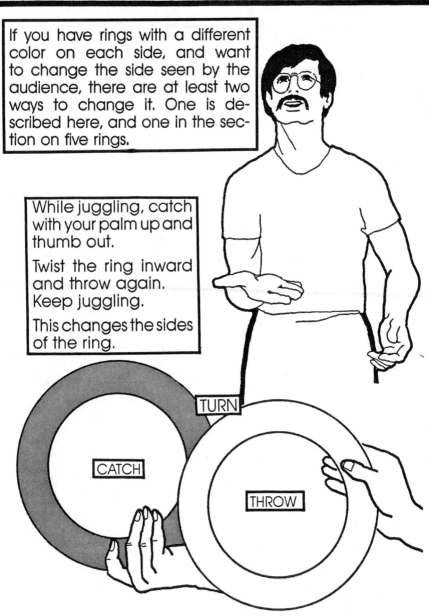

CATCH

TURN

THROW

SPINNING THE RING

To spin a ring on a ring, pinch the spinner ring with the fingers of your dominant hand.

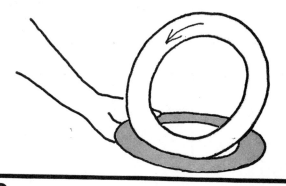

TIP
Don't throw high—instead, "Snap" your wrist.

If you are facing the audience, you can turn the
rings so they are flat in front of you.

NOTE

YOU CAN FLIP THEM LIKE PANCAKES

CLUB JUGGLING

BARRETT FELKER

GETTING STARTED

KNOB

HANDLE

BULB

BUTT

HOLD THE CLUB LEVEL IN YOUR RIGHT HAND AT A 45° ANGLE AWAY FROM YOUR BODY. PLACE YOUR THUMB WHERE THE HANDLE BEGINS TO WIDEN.

THROWING ONE CLUB

CLUB JUGGLING REQUIRES A SMOOTH "SCOOP" ACTION. THE BUTT OF THE CLUB MAKES A "U" IN THE AIR.

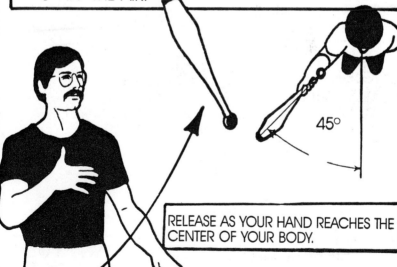

45°

RELEASE AS YOUR HAND REACHES THE CENTER OF YOUR BODY.

71

AIM HERE AT FIRST,

2 FEET

THEN AFTER A FEW THROWS COME DOWN SLOWLY. EVENTUALLY THE ENTIRE PATTERN TAKES PLACE BELOW EYE LEVEL.

THE CLUB SHOULD MAKE A SINGLE FLIP AND END UP POINTING TO THE LEFT AT A 45° ANGLE.

NOW, REPEAT FROM LEFT TO RIGHT. WHEN YOU HAVE A GOOD TOSS IN BOTH DIRECTIONS, MOVE ON TO THE NEXT STEP

EXCHANGING 2 CLUBS

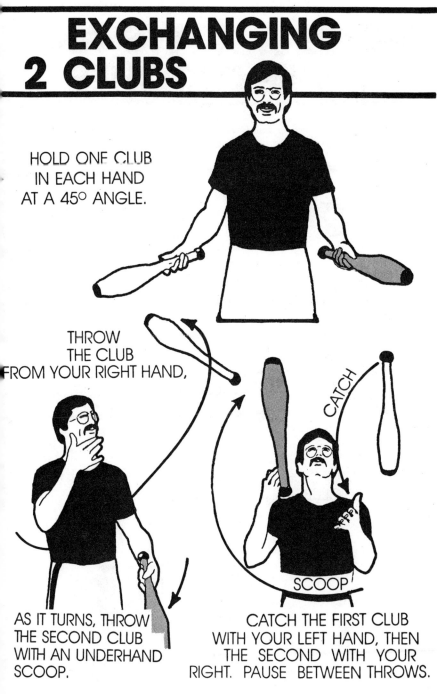

HOLD ONE CLUB IN EACH HAND AT A 45° ANGLE.

THROW THE CLUB FROM YOUR RIGHT HAND,

CATCH

SCOOP

AS IT TURNS, THROW THE SECOND CLUB WITH AN UNDERHAND SCOOP.

CATCH THE FIRST CLUB WITH YOUR LEFT HAND, THEN THE SECOND WITH YOUR RIGHT. PAUSE BETWEEN THROWS.

73

THREE THROWS AND THREE CATCHES

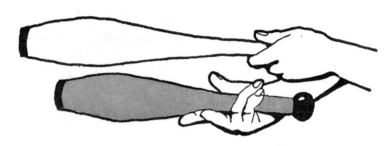

HOLD ONE CLUB IN EACH HAND, AND PLACE AN ADDITIONAL CLUB IN THE RIGHT HAND...

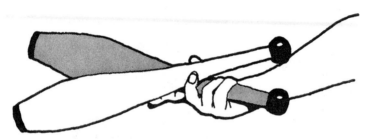

WITH YOUR INDEX FINGER EXTENDED ALONG THE NECK OF THE CLUB.

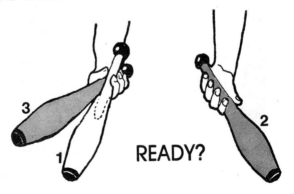

READY?

THROW CLUB NO. 1, WHEN IT TURNS, THROW CLUB NO. 2.

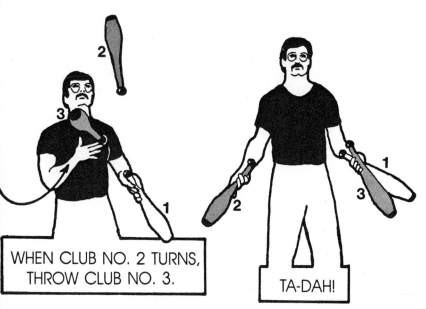

WHEN CLUB NO. 2 TURNS, THROW CLUB NO. 3.

TA-DAH!

75

CONTINUOUS JUGGLING

REMEMBER!

JUGGLE HIGH WHEN YOU FIRST LEARN, IT GIVES YOU MORE TIME.

NOW EVERY TIME ONE CLUB SPINS, THROW ANOTHER. KEEP ALTERNATING: RIGHT-LEFT, RIGHT-LEFT.

EVENTUALLY, YOU SHOULD LOOK OVER THE TOP OF YOUR PATTERN.

AS YOU INCREASE YOUR SKILLS, BRING YOUR PATTERN DOWN SO THE CLUBS GO NO HIGHER THAN THE TOP OF YOUR HEAD.

HERE'S SOME TIPS FOR CONSISTENT CLUB JUGGLING

Get good scoops. Try to throw the clubs about a foot over the shoulder on each side, no higher. You should eventually be able to bring the pattern down and to bring your eyes down to the point where you can look directly ahead. This will be important when you start passing clubs. You want to look straight ahead, at your partner's eyes, not up in the air. Now learn to catch half spins and one and a half spins, regaining your pattern from the erratic throws. Relax your arms and shoulders. Keep your hands down, with your forearms parallel to the floor. As time goes by, use less shoulder and upper arm to throw the clubs, and use more wrist and forearm. Experiment with the use of your thumb to push down on the handle, giving the club faster spin and reducing your effort even further.

HAVING SOME PROBLEMS?

Q. WHY DO MY CLUBS COLLIDE?
A. 1. YOUR PATTERN IS NOT WIDE ENOUGH. EXTEND
      YOUR "SCOOP", OR . . .
   2. YOUR TIMING IS OFF—BE SURE ONE CLUB HAS PEAKED
      WHEN THE NEXT CLUB IS THROWN.

Q. I'VE MOVED ON TO 3 CLUBS, AND NOW I CAN'T CATCH
   ANYTHING.
A. TOO MUCH SPIN OR NOT ENOUGH SPIN — GO BACK TO
   ONE CLUB AND BUILD UP YOUR PRECISION

Q. MY CLUBS ARE "RUNNING AWAY" FROM ME.
A. REMEMBER JUGGLING TAKES PLACE IN A PLANE IN FRONT
   OF YOU. IMPROVE YOUR SCOOPS AND THROWS FROM SIDE
   TO SIDE.

Q. MY CLUBS ARE ATTACKING ME. I KEEP GETTING HIT IN THE
   CHEST.
A. STAND YOUR GROUND AND THROW SIDE TO SIDE — DON'T
   BACK UP.

FOR EXTRA CREDIT

UNDER THE LEG

*IN ORDER TO THROW A CLUB UNDER THE LEG, START WITH A SINGLE CLUB.

LEARN TO THROW THAT ONE CLUB UNDER THE RIGHT AND LEFT LEG FROM THE RIGHT AND LEFT HAND.

YOU CAN THROW UNDER THE SAME, OR . . . OPPOSITE LEG.

NOW TRY THE MOVE WHILE JUGGLING. START BY THROWING EVERY THIRD CLUB UNDER. IT MAY HELP TO TOSS THE PREVIOUS ONE A BIT HIGHER THAN USUAL TO GIVE SOME EXTRA TIME. TRY EVERY SECOND CLUB, THEN CONTINUOUS THROWS WITH ONE HAND.

FLOATERS

THE CLUB DOESN'T FLIP AT ALL. HOLD THE CLUB HIGH ON THE NECK AND SPIN IT A BIT FOR STABILITY.

REVERSE SPIN

THE HANDLE
GOES UP
AND AWAY FROM YOU.

PUSH THE KNOB END OF THE CLUB UP AND AWAY FROM YOU. THIS REQUIRES A GOOD DEAL OF FORCE, AND SEEMS AWKWARD AT FIRST, BUT EVENTUALLY CAN BE AS EASY AS NORMAL SINGLE SPINS.

BALANCING

BALANCE ONE CLUB ON YOUR CHIN OR NOSE, PAUSE AND DROP IT BACK INTO THE JUGGLE.

BEHIND THE BACK

NOTE

DOUBLE FLIPS WORK TOO!

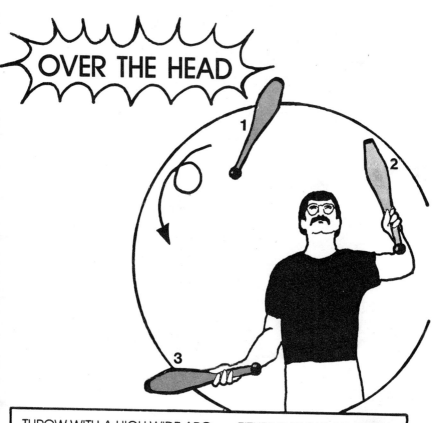

OVER THE HEAD

THROW WITH A HIGH WIDE ARC . . . EITHER DOUBLE OR SINGLE FLIP.

HOW TO GET HOT

★ SEVERAL HOURS PRACTICE A DAY ARE RECOMMENDED.
★ KEEP A RECORD OF PRACTICE SESSIONS.
★ STRIVE TO DO MORE EACH TIME YOU PICK UP THE EQUIPMENT.
★ YOUR MOTIVATION MUST COME FROM WITHIN.

KICK UPS

IN ORDER TO PICK UP A CLUB WITH A "KICK-UP", PRACTICE BY SETTING THE CLUB ON YOUR FOOT. THE HANDLE SHOULD POINT INWARD AND REST ON THE AREA BETWEEN YOUR FOOT AND SHIN. FLEX YOUR FOOT AS YOU KICK UP AND BACK. THE KNOB OF THE CLUB SHOULD CATCH YOUR SHIN AND THE CLUB SHOULD DO A SINGLE FLIP TO YOUR HAND.

REMEMBER

IN ORDER TO KEEP YOUR CLUBS IN GOOD SHAPE, THE BEST AREAS TO JUGGLE ARE:
A PADDED FLOOR, CARPETED AREA, GYM MATS OR A CLEAN, DRY LAWN.

STYLE

Shoulders up,
throwing with entire
arm

Shoulders down
and relaxed, using
wrist to throw.

QUESTION

Which looks better? You be the judge.

PERFORMING

PUTTING TOGETHER A ROUTINE

Not everyone who juggles wants to perform. Even so, it is important to learn the transitions between tricks and to find ways to maintain the flow of objects. Being able to move smoothly from trick to trick makes your own juggling more interesting to you and helps you learn new moves.

If you have individual moves and series of moves under control, you can weave them together to make a routine. Instead of practicing individual tricks, you practice a series of moves that have a particular flow to them; you practice them over and over, concentrating not on the moves themselves but on the smooth transition from one trick to another.

In putting your routine together, there are two paths you can follow—with or without musical accompaniment. If you want to juggle to music, pick a piece that has some changes of tempo or one that fits your juggling style. First you get the feel of the piece by juggling with your chosen music in the background. Eventually you will feel more comfortable doing certain tricks at certain times. That's when you start putting your moves into a sequence and practicing them in that sequence over and over to the music.

Symphonic overtures (like *William Tell*), swing-era jazz tunes (*A Train*), ragtime (*Maple Leaf Rag*), Tijuana Brass, TV and movie themes, and rock and roll can all be appropriate. You will probably find instrumental versions less distracting for the audience than vocal renditions.

To fit your juggling to the music, remember that you not only have a list of tricks from which to choose, but that these tricks can be done higher, wider and more slowly or tighter, smaller and more quickly, and that you can use the height and breadth of your stage as well. You can use minimal arm movements or big swinging motions. You can incorporate movement from side to side, turns and spins, leaps and acrobatics into your routine. You can sit, kneel or stand. Rastelli lay down to juggle, and Bobby May stood on his head. You can surprise the audience with a high throw out of a low pattern, a bounced ball that goes away and comes back again, movement of your head from side to side, an abrupt kick, a bounce off the forehead or bicep or even a sudden stop, balancing a ball on your forehead or a club on your foot. If your music is full of surprises, your juggling should be also. If your music is lyrical or driving or silly, so should your juggling be.

Use a friend, a mirror or, best of all, a video camera to look at your routine. Remember that a routine has highs and lows. Your first trick should be impressive, and your last should be a crowd-pleaser, but in between you want some applause points to give the audience a chance to show their appreciation.

When you decide to put together a routine *without* musical accompaniment, you can perform in silence or you can join the ranks of talking jugglers. Comedic patter may appear easy, but it requires the same discipline as a tightly scripted musical routine and the same attention to tempo. Now, however, we call it "timing."

Often a juggling trick reminds you of something else—a yo-yo, a tennis match, a volcano. So use a few of the easy ones that already have names. Generally speaking, you name the trick at the moment audience recognition takes place. In other words, you say "The juggler's Yo-Yo" just as you begin to do it. If you start doing it first, people will titter and giggle, and this noise may drown out your pronouncement. If you announce the trick too soon, the element of surprise is reduced. The verbal and visual images should register on the brain of the audience members simultaneously.

Also, the order in which you present "silly stuff" is important. For instance, you announce "Juggler's Tennis" and use as much of the stage as you can, running from side to side doing that trick. Each time you throw a long one you say, "Smash" or, "It's a long one." Suddenly you throw one to center stage and do the same move tightly, look up and say, "Fast volley at the net," toss one high and say "Lob," throw it off stage and say "Lost ball." If you drop, it's "Love—15."

In comedy juggling, keep your words to a minimum. You generally do the setup verbally, then the objects you are juggling deliver your punch line. Don't forget that you can accentuate your comedy juggling with funny faces or postures that reinforce the moves.

Silent juggling can be both musical and comic, since the audience will hear the music of your hands slapping the equipment, and you can use facial expressions and the element of surprise to elicit laughter. With a devil stick, or three clubs with sleigh bells taped on them, or cigar boxes, diabolos or torches you can use the noise made by the equipment to create a beat.

GUIDELINES FROM THE GREATS

Now let's look at a few of the guidelines the great jugglers of the past have given us. The combined wisdom of Francis and Lottie Brunn, Nick Gatto, Bobby May, Homer Stack and Enrico Rastelli provides some rules an aspiring performer ignores at great risk.

1. Practice every day for 20 minutes (Stack), one hour (Gatto), two hours (May) or as much as you can (Brunn, Brunn and Rastelli).

2. Count your repetitions of difficult moves and always do more than you did in the previous practice session.

3. Practice your routine over and over again from start to finish, until you can perform without any drops.

4. Don't copy other jugglers; instead, look at other art forms for your inspiration, such as dance, acrobatics, theater, comedy or music.

5. Use your entire body and plenty of variety in your juggling to cover the entire stage, just as a painter covers an entire canvas.

6. Use costuming, makeup, lighting, stage props and assistants to give your act a well-prepared, clean, polished look.

7. Develop a stage character and juggle in character.

8. Project vitality and enthusiasm with your body and your face. Smile and have fun. If you do, the audience will enjoy themselves too.

PRESENTATION

As a performer, you want to have as much control as possible over the environment in which you perform. Sometimes you will have to work under severely restricted conditions. The ceiling of the cruise ship may be so low that you have to omit your flashy start. The corner of the room in the comedy club may be lit by a single blinding spotlight. The circus may have three rings full of jugglers and be playing the other guy's music. The only half-decent street corner in town may be next to a major bus stop. But when you can find a good spot or a good stage, you can make it a great experience for your audience.

If it is your show from the opening curtain to the final act, start by making sure that the audience is comfortable and everybody can see and hear you. As they come in, if it is in character to do so, you might greet them and start to make friends before the show starts.

If possible, music should play in the background as your audience assembles. Show tunes, movie or TV themes or circus music will each set a different mood. Try them all and see which one suits you.

If there is a curtain, have it closed and direct every light you have on it. Someone introduces you, the house lights dim, the curtain opens, and all your butterflies flutter away as you meet your audience.

Here you have a decision to make. You can start out already standing on stage, or you can come on in character. Are you a comic juggler? Perhaps you want to walk on slowly. Are you a speedy Las Vegas–style performer? You may run in juggling to fast music. No matter how you come onto the stage and no matter how primitive that stage may be, take the time to stop, look slowly around the room (the street corner, the field, the beach), smile and make eye contact. A bow, a wave, or "Hi, everybody" may be appropriate. Acknowledge the audience.

Once that first contact has been made, you can proceed with the show, but give the audience frequent opportunities to release their tension through laughter, applause or both, and acknowledge their appreciation. Nod your head, say thanks, look directly at them and speak in a natural voice. As someone once said, "Pretend you are playing to that one little buckaroo."

I like to think of a performance as a string of jewels. The performer's task is to polish and perfect each jewel and string them in an order that is esthetically pleasing. Old vaudevillians used to say, "Don't try to follow a banjo act with a banjo act," and in our necklace analogy it makes sense to balance your gems, not lump all of the same type together.

Whether you present an eight-minute circus-style show or an hour or more of material, you need to vary the presentation to keep interest high. You can use different kinds of equipment. You can bring on your partner, and he or she can do a solo number or the two of you can juggle together. You can alternate comedy and musical numbers. Bring a volunteer or two on stage or go out into the audience yourself. A number under black lights with fluorescent equipment, torch swinging or juggling, the use of apparently dangerous equipment, madcap antics, a lyrical number with scarves to ballet music, a balance routine or a chase scene can all be strung together in a logical order. With some forethought you may even be able to weave a story line through the whole show. If not, there should be some consistent threads of style, characterization and/or running gags that help tie all your baubles together.

NOVELTY ROUTINES IN THE PUBLIC DOMAIN

When you are first starting out, you need some material. Fortunately, there are many routines in the public domain. Some are classic moves, like changing the color of juggling rings or eating an apple while juggling, and these are included in their respective chapters. Others are bits of lore from vaudeville days. A partial list includes:

Apple and a Fork

Balance a fork on the back of your hand with the handle running up your forearm. Hold an apple in your hand, fingers pointed down around the apple. Bring your hand up quickly, tossing the apple and look up simultaneously. Quickly withdraw your hand, catch the handle of the fork and spear the apple as it comes down.

Apple and Fork (Audience Participation Version)

Build up the handle of a fork with wood and wrap it with foam tape to make it soft. Toss an apple (or a turnip) into the audience. Tell them that it is an old vaudeville tradition to toss fruit at performers. Have them throw with a high lob, and catch the fruit on the fork, which you hold in your teeth.

Ball on a String

Attach a piece of thread or nylon fishing line that blends in with your costume to one ball. Tie the other end of the string to your belt buckle. Juggle three balls and drop that one. It swings between your legs and back up into the pattern.

Musical Juggling

Tambourines can be juggled like rings and slapped on your hip or knee while juggling. Sleigh bells can be tied together in clusters and juggled like balls, or taped to clubs for a special Christmas effect. Of course you can juggle balls off of a drumhead, or use heavy drumsticks which can be juggled in various patterns while you play the drums. Several vaudeville-era jugglers could keep three or more banjos going and play a tune on them at the same time.

Tennis Theme

There are a number of tennis variations. One is to juggle a ball, the can the balls came in and a racket. For a finale, catch the can, catch the racket, hit the ball with the racket, and catch the ball in the can. Many jugglers use tennis rackets the way others use clubs. Buy the most inexpensive rackets you can find. You might as well go all the way and use a tennis outfit for this routine. You can balance a tennis racket on your chin while juggling three tennis balls. Or you can hit a tennis racket back and forth with two hand sticks, just like a devil stick.

Parasol Work

Get a Chinese or Japanese parasol made of coated paper and experiment with the following: balancing the parasol on its handle or on the rim; juggling the parasol and two other objects; spinning the handle of the opened parasol in one hand while a large ball or a rubber quoit circles around on the top. (Hint—Hold the top of the parasol at eye level, tilt it away slightly and gently roll the ball against the direction of the turn.) You can "gimmick" the ball by attaching it by a string to the top of the parasol, but you may as well put in the time to learn the move.

Ball on the Nose

Coat a Ping-Pong ball with rubber cement. Put rubber cement on the end of your nose. After a suitable buildup and a drum roll, toss the Ping-Pong ball high in the air, tilt your head back and let it hit your nose. It will stick there. For a few seconds you seem to be balancing the Ping-Pong ball on your nose. The audience bursts into spontaneous applause. Then tilt your head forward so they can see that the ball is stuck to your nose.

Juggling Blindfolded

It is possible to juggle blindfolded, and practicing this skill will help you to be a more precise juggler. It will also help you to stay in control when blinded by spotlights. However, there are blindfolds that can be bought in magic stores, through which you can see perfectly. For a comedy routine, you tie on a blindfold and juggle with your right side to the audience. After they are suitably impressed, you turn toward them and they see that there is a hole cut in the blindfold for your left eye.

Giving Yourself Awards

When you do a particularly good trick you can get out your diploma and display it on your prop case. When you miss, go over to the case and turn the diploma face down. Pin a medal just inside the handkerchief pocket of your jacket. When you execute a good trick, pull out the medal so it hangs in front of the pocket. Later, when you miss, tuck it back into the pocket. When you do a really good trick, open your jacket to reveal a large number of medals pinned on the inside.

Balancing a Paper Cone

Roll a sheet of newspaper into a cone shape. Soak the lower five or six inches of the cone in heavily salted water. Then let it dry. In your act, light the upper end and balance the burning cone on your nose, forehead or chin. The rising heat will help you to balance the cone until it burns all the way down to the salted portion. (Warning—Perform this trick only where there is a high ceiling and no wind. Kids perform under adult supervision only, please.)

Hat and Stick Tricks

If you have a soft, floppy round hat made of felt or canvas, you can keep it spinning vertically in front of you by hitting upward on the outside edge of the brim with a stick about two feet long. The "hit" gives the hat enough momentum to keep spinning and enough lift to keep it aloft. Combine this with ideas from the plate-spinning and hat-manipulation chapters to put together a unique act.

Coin Tricks

Start by juggling three 50-cent pieces or silver dollars. Toss one flat so it lands on your forehead. (Charles Carrer could slide a coin from this position onto his eye, where it became a "monocle." Ginquevalli is said to have been able to kick a coin directly from the tip of his toe to be caught on his eye as a monocle.) Line the three coins up on the back of your hand and wrist. Toss the coins into the air and catch them in three quick clawing motions with the same hand. Put a long line of coins on the back of your forearm; toss them all up and catch them in one forward swoop with that hand.

Palm Rolling

Start with two bumper pool balls. Turn them around one another in the palm of one hand, then learn with the other hand. Next, learn to send three balls around in a circle in each hand. In general, your thumb does most of the work pushing the balls around. If you tilt your hands forward, gravity will help. Now learn to "weave" three, five and seven balls by allowing them to roll from hand to hand in an infinity sign pattern. This can also be done with eight balls, which turn like interlocking gears, or with nine balls, which weave from hand to hand.

Magic and Juggling

There was a time when magic and juggling were much closer, but with the increase in recreational juggling, the two art forms have diverged. In magic stores you can find devices and books that describe methods for producing your juggling props "from thin air." Your juggling scarves, for instance, can come out of an apparently empty coin purse. Your juggling balls can appear in a production tube and disappear in a collapsing box. Look in the Yellow Pages under "Magicians' Supplies" to find your nearest magic store.

Croquet Ball off the Head

Show the audience three balls which are apparently the same. Drop one or two on the floor with a thud. Explain that these are "rock-hard croquet balls" and that you will toss one high into the air and bounce it off your head. After a few false starts, toss one high up and let it bounce off your head with a resounding "crack." Actually, the ball that bounces off your head is a hollow rubber ball. They are all wrapped in plastic tape to look similar. The noise is caused by hitting the actual croquet balls together as the rubber ball bounces off your forehead.

Hoop Juggling

Plastic "Hula Hoops" can be used for a number of tricks. While juggling them, toss one across the floor with reverse spin. It will return, and you can resume juggling just as it gets to you. Or roll all three away from you with reverse spin, one at a time, and juggle them on the floor in this manner, using both hands. Experiment with rolling the hoops across your back, or rolling one away with reverse spin, pointing your toe in the path of its return, and allowing it to roll up your leg and back into the juggling pattern.

Hat, Cane and Cigar

One common trick in vaudeville days was to balance a hat and cigar on the foot, as shown. The cigar was actually made of wood. You kick the hat to your head and the cigar to your mouth in a single move. Some jugglers spiced up this trick by adding a whisk broom, which went into the jacket pocket (held open with a wire loop), or a cane, which ended up in the hand.

Raid the Equipment Locker

If a school show takes place in the gym, you can run into the equipment room and toss out whatever you find: a plastic baseball bat, Hula Hoops, traffic cones, bowling pins, basketballs, etc. Run through them quickly, showing how they can all be juggled, then toss them back and close the door. The entire routine can be done in three minutes.

97

Rubber Chickens

You can do a hilarious routine with three rubber chickens, which can be bought in any magic store. Put a dowel through the chicken from head to tail and secure it with a nail. Now think of all the fowl humor you can: "Don't be chicken." "Only a dumb cluck wants to lay an egg." "The yolk's on the audience." Of course, chickens are flying in a passing pattern while the patter flies back and forth as well. For variety add a plastic fish or a rubber dolphin to this act: "Something fishy here, folks."

Egg and Plate

This trick takes plenty of practice. You will break some eggs. A metal plate works best. During practice you may want to cover the plate with a layer of foam-backed tape. Once you have the knack, remove the tape.

The trick is simple enough. You toss an egg into the air and catch it on the plate. However, to keep it from breaking, you must absorb the shock by cushioning the fall with a scooping catch.

After you have tossed and caught the egg several times, going higher each time, you can deliberately fail to cushion the fall, and let the egg crash on the plate.

Egg Juggling

Call a volunteer up on stage. Have him choose three eggs from a carton. Explain that you will be juggling the three eggs, but at a certain point in time you will toss the third egg to your volunteer. Now run around the audience juggling the eggs. If they are seated on the floor or on the ground, so much the better. Warn them to move away when you come near. Children will shriek.

For your finale, toss the third egg high up for your volunteer. Holding your two eggs high, go back to the stage and break your eggs into a jar. Have your volunteer do the same, to prove that you were not using fake or hard-boiled eggs.

Eating an Apple

Eating an apple while juggling it is relatively easy. The trick is to do it with style. This may mean eating mixed fruit (an apple, a pear and a peach). It may mean eating fast and very sloppily so that the apple dribbles down your shirt front. It may mean eating a balanced meal of an item from the vegetable group (a cucumber), one from the grain group (a whole wheat roll) and one from the protein group (a mozzarella cheese).

To learn to eat while juggling, simply bring the item to your mouth before tossing it. If you can kiss it, you can bite it. Practice with a beanbag. Then try an apple. Learn to bite from both the right and left hands.

Taking a Bow

If you are juggling three rings, toss one high with a pancake flip, catch it around your neck and hold out your arms with one ring in each hand. Your audience will automatically applaud. If you catch a beanbag on your neck in a deep bow they will applaud also. What are they responding to? Body position.

Some performers, like Francis Brunn, continually punctuate their acts with striking poses. Others flow through without a pause and take their bow at the end, depriving the audience of a release for their tension. Poses should become second nature to you. Practice looking in a mirror. When you catch that last beanbag, stretch your arm out to its full length. While juggling four balls, casually cross one foot over the other in a pose of supreme ease. Or hold your three clubs like a bouquet of flowers at the end of your routine.

The art of taking a bow is an important one to master. It is tempting to bow once, turn and run out. But remember your character. If you just finished a funny routine, walk out funny. If you were flashy, you can run out, but wave goodby as you do, and you'll probably get a curtain call. Keep your body turned toward the audience and your smile bright and shining until you are fully off stage.

SHOWMANSHIP

Showmanship is often more important than skill, and confidence in your character is a key element in developing it. It is gained through practice and paying attention to the messages your audiences give you.

Jugglers have an enhanced opportunity to develop showmanship because of their fallibility. You can memorize the lines of a play or rehearse a song over and over until it is perfect and then present it without a fault. Even if you miss a line or forget a word or two, the audience probably won't notice. But when you drop a juggling prop, everyone sees it.

If you have developed showmanship, after the performance people will say, "Did you drop that on purpose?" or, "I really liked it when you pretended to miss and dropped that club." What they mean is, your recovery was so natural, or so funny, that they thought it was part of the show.

To accomplish this miracle, be relaxed. Don't rush your recovery. Make it part of your routine with a witty line or a "cover-up" move. Drop lines include:

- "Three tries for the hard ones!"

- "A sudden gust of gravity!"

- "Someone in the front row moved his foot!"

- "I just washed my hands, and I can't do a thing with them!"

- "The sun got in my eyes!"

- "Nobody noticed!"

- "Almost dropped one!"

- "That one's yours!" (If it goes into the audience.)

- "Don't worry, it's part of the show!"

- "That's my floor show!"

Cover-up moves include:

- Dropping to your knees and picking up the prop while still juggling.

- Having an audience member toss the prop back into the pattern.

- Throwing all three things down and doing something else for a while, then coming back to the fallen props.

- Going to your prop stand and getting something funny, like a book that says *How to Juggle* in big letters, a gigantic pair of eyeglasses or a gun to shoot the fallen item.

- Starting to do another trick. For instance, if you drop one club, start swinging the other two.

- Kicking the prop back up into your pattern.

Soon you will find you are inventing your own lines and your own cover-ups to fit your character.

A NOTE ON PLAGIARISM

Juggling has been around for so long that it is hard to prove that anyone "invented" anything. This is particularly true when you use relatively standard props and follow someone else's formula. This book is not intended to produce thousands of "copy-cat" jugglers who all do the same generic juggling show. They key ingredients in creating something of your own are imagination and experimentation.

Certain routines are so strongly identified with one person or group that if anyone else were to do them there would be an immediate outcry from other jugglers. Certainly there is nothing wrong with using the same kind of equipment as a fellow juggler, or performing in a particular style, or assuming a vaguely similar character or appearance. However, when these characteristics all add up to an overt copy of the other person's lines or costume or manner of speaking, you have crossed the boundary.

For example, the Flying Karamazov Brothers (FKB) perform a number of unique routines. If any other juggling troop urges their audience to bring difficult items from home "larger than an ounce and smaller than a breadbox" and has their "champ" attempt to juggle them or suffer a pie in the face as a penalty, that troop should at the very least publicly attribute the invention of that particular routine to the FKB.

If a solo performer juggles a bowling ball, an apple and an egg, eats the apple while juggling, and ends up smashing the egg into his face, he is directly copying Michael Davis and should get his permission or refrain from doing the trick. If a juggler were to affect the voice and mannerisms of W. C. Fields, dress in a top hat and imitate Fields' routines, he would be in jeopardy of a suit by the heirs who hold the copyright to the routines of W. C. Fields.

As you develop as a performer, don't hesitate to learn as much technical juggling as you can. Technical skill is in the public domain. But create your own style and your own imaginative routines.

SCHOOL ASSEMBLIES

Because school assemblies are the "bread and butter" of so many jugglers, I include the guidelines developed by the Juggling Institute to help you in planning a school-assembly program.

1. Get to the school at least an hour before the show and let them know you have arrived.

2. Give the principal an introduction to read and help him or her rehearse it.

3. Make the space in which you will be performing look as much like a theater as possible. This may mean using some sort of backdrop, sweeping the stage or the gym floor, and using curtains, lights and a good sound system, if available. If you are in a secondary school with bleachers on both sides of the gym, use one side only.

4. Play upbeat non-rock music as the students come into the room. Movie or TV themes or show tunes work to set the mood well.

5. Greet the students at the door. Shake hands, make eye contact, chat with them.

6. If you have your choice between seating the students on the floor or in chairs, always opt for the floor. It will make the audience more compact, quieter and easier to control.

7. Don't practice or warm up in front of your audience.

8. You may, however, do some "business" as the students file in. Play with the younger kids or with a broom or with your hat. This gets everyone excited and makes friends for you.

9. Again, after you are in front of the group, make solid eye contact with as many students as you can.

10. Have the principal or a student leader give you a solid introduction. We use: "They've toured the world—they've

been on many TV shows—now here they are at _____ School, *alive* and *in person*, Professor Confidence and Amy from the Juggling Institute."

11. Run in enthusiastically and acknowledge the applause.

12. Once the show begins, ask questions of the entire group at appropriate times in the show: "How many of you have tried to learn to juggle?" "How many have succeeded?"

13. Sometimes you may want one person to answer. Simply say, "Let's see a hand. Who knows _____?"

14. If you need a volunteer but the audience is getting noisy, say, "We have a special way of choosing volunteers. We pick the person who sits quietly and makes the funniest face," or, "We pick the person who wiggles his or her nose the best."

15. Touch the volunteer on the hands, back or shoulders in a reassuring manner as he or she joins you.

16. If you bring a member of the audience on stage, make sure he or she leaves as a hero.

17. Play to the teachers as well as the students.

18. Don't patronize or use a "special voice" for children. Play to the upper grades so the lower ones will have to stretch to keep up, but don't play so far over their heads that they get bored.

19. Keep up the pace of the show. There should never be a dull moment.

20. At every opportunity, make teaching points about topics such as:

    a. Diet and nutrition
    b. Making friends
    c. Exercise and learning new skills
    d. Helping each other to learn

e. Sticking to tasks until finished
f. Accepting challenges
g. Being different is OK
h. Anti-smoking or alcohol
i. Math, spelling, English, foreign languages

21. Drama training helps. Here are a few simple rules:

a. Face the audience and, when turning your body, keep looking toward them.

b. When your partner is alone on stage or making a presentation, stay out of sight. Avoid upstaging each other.

c. Warm up backstage with easy tricks. There should be no audible drops coming from backstage.

d. When lighting is limited, focus it on one spot and play in that spot.

e. Wear costumes that set you apart from the rest of the world and make a statement such as "This is an athlete" (tennis outfit or muscle shirt), "This is a person with dignity" (three-piece suit for men, evening dress for women), "This is a star" (sequins, strong basic colors such as black, red or white, gold and silver), "This is a clown" (silly shoes or hat, old-fashioned clothes).

f. Develop a character and stay in that character.

g. Most of all, teach them to be a good audience.

Audience Training

Because you will be called upon to perform for school groups, you should learn these two methods of audience control which work well, with young people or any group in a theatrical setting.

Making Rain

Say to the audience, "Do as I do." Then show them your two index fingers, and tap the fingers together lightly. Hold up your index and middle fingers and tap them together. Hold up your first three fingers and tap them. Display your four fingers and tap them. Finally, hold up your hands and hit them together in a full burst of applause. Now work your way back down to four, three, two and one finger and finally to none. At that point you should have full attention and absolute silence. Then shout "Cloudburst!" hold up both hands and start clapping furiously. Then one finger again and silence. Now whenever the audience gets a bit noisy, simply say "Cloudburst!" and start clapping. Then go to one finger and silence. It works every time.

Hi! Hi! Hi!

Come on stage in silence. Wave to the audience and mime "Hi!" Someone will say "Hi!" to you. Mime "Hi!" back to them and encourage them to say it back to you by a thumbs up signal and/or by cupping your hands behind your ears. Now alternate with them. You mime "Hi!" and they say "Hi!" back. Now split the audience in half by indicating one side of the room. Signal that side to be quiet. Say "Hi!" to the other side. Hold your hand up palm down and wiggle it from side to side to show that that's OK but not great. Now signal to that half of the room to be quiet and get the other half to shout "Hi!" Show your pleasure at this. Now alternate back and forth from side to side, by raising one arm, then the other. Finally raise both arms together for everyone to shout "Hi!" You can start doing jumping jacks, and everyone will laugh together. Put your palms down and signal for silence. Later in the show, when you want silence, use that signal again. The principle at work here is strange. If you want the audience to be quiet, first make them noisy.

APPENDIX 1:
RESOURCES AND ADDRESSES

To order retail quantities of juggling equipment by mail, ask for a juggling equipment catalog from:

California Juggling Institute, PO Box 15845, Santa Ana, CA 92705 (714) 541-5845

Cascade Juggling, 474 Enniskillen Ave., Winnipeg, Manitoba, Canada R2V 0J4 (204) 586-5785

Illinois Juggling Institute, 143 N. Pershing, Bensenville, IL 60106 (800) 766-1437

JUGGLEBUG, Inc., 7526J Olympic View Drive, Edmonds, WA 98026 (800) 523-1776

The Jugglers' Club, 120 E. Palmer Ave., Collingswood, NJ 08108 (800) I-JUGGLE

Hank Lee's Magic Factory, PO Box 789, Medford, MA 02155 (617) 482-8749

Louis Tannen, Inc., 6 West 32nd St, New York 10001 (212) 239-8383

Or you can get a catalog that includes juggling equipment along with other products, usually for a small fee, from any of the following:

Abbott's Magic Co., Colon, MI 49040 (616) 432-3235

Hank Lee's Magic Factory, PO Box 789, Medford, MA 02155 (617) 482-8749

Hollywood Magic, 6614 Hollywood Blvd., Hollywood, CA 90028 (213) 464-5610

Ickle Pickle Products, 883 Somerton Ridge Dr., St. Louis, MO 63141 (314) 434-3630

Klutz Products, PO Box 2992, Stanford, CA 94305 (415) 857-0888

Louis Tannen, Inc., 6 West 32nd St, New York 10001 (212) 239-8383

US Toy Company, 2008 West 103rd Terrace, Leawood, KS 66206 (913) 642-8247

World Footbag Assn., 1317 Washington Ave., #7, Golden, CO 80401 (303) 278-9797

Whether you shop for juggling equipment by mail or buy juggling props at your local magic, toy or sporting good store, look for the JUGGLEBUG® label, your assurance of quality in juggling products. *The Joy of Juggling - The Video* is a thirty minute tape that follows the same general plan as the instructional portion of this book. *Juggling Step by Step* is a two hour video version of our 576 page instructional book, *The Complete Juggler*. Our award winning children's instructional video series includes three titles, JUGGLETIME™, JUGGLING STAR™ and JUGGLER'S JAM™, presenting a total of thirty five children's music videos. If you enjoy this book and are interested in the philisophical and spiritual side of your juggling self, look for *The Zen of Juggling*, by the author of this book. Check your local book store or library. All of these books and videos are available through the sources mentioned above. If you can't find a specific title, contact JUGGLEBUG, 7526J Olympic View Drive, Edmonds, WA 98026, (206) 774-2127.

Classroom teachers or physical educators who want to start a juggling program for their students can call The Juggling Institute in Edmonds Washington at (800) 523-1776 and request a free loan copy of *Juggling for Success at Hazel Dell School*. This fifteen minute documentary tells the story of one school where students take frequent juggling breaks throughout the day in the classroom. In this video Hazel Dell teachers explain that the impact on student physical fitness, self-esteem, school spirit, academic performance and deportment has been profound. This video can be your "sales tool" to get your principal and fellow teachers to participate in a school-wide juggling program.

If you want to get an institutional catalog to order juggling equipment in quantity for physical education or recreation programs, contact any of the following:

	Local #	800 #
Bill Fritz Sports	(919) 362-1748	(800) 234-1004
BSN Corporation	(214) 484-9484	(800) 292-7772
Chime Time	(404) 449-5700	(800) 444-5700
Flaghouse	(914) 699-2961	(800) 221-5185
Gopher Athletics	(507) 451-7470	(800) 533-0446
Greg Larson Sports	(218) 829-5358	(800) 950-3320
Gym Closet	(313) 852-7333	(800) 445-8873
Illinois Juggling Inst	(788) 766-1437	(800) 766-1437
JUGGLEBUG,INC	(206) 774-2127	(800) 523-1776
Palos Sports	(708) 448-6222	(800) 233-5484
Passon's Sports	(214) 484-9484	(800) 292-7772
Physical Educators	(718) 258-7333	
School Tech	(313) 761-5173	(800) 521-2832
Snitz Manufacturing	(414) 642-3991	(800) 558-2224
Sportime	(404) 449-5700	(800) 444-5700
Things From Bell	(414) 642-7337	(800) 558-2224
Toledo PE Supply	(419) 476-6730	(800) 225-7749
US Games	(214) 484-9484	(800) 292-7772

If you own a store or a catalog company and want to carry a few items or a full line of juggling equipment, contact:

D. Robbins & Co., Inc., 70 Washington St., Brooklyn, NY 11201 (718) 625-1804

Ickle Pickle Products, 883 Somerton Ridge Dr., St. Louis, MO 63141 (314) 434-3630

JUGGLEBUG, 7506J Olympic View Drive, Edmonds, WA 98026 (800) 523-1776

Magic City, 15528 Illinois Ave., Paramount, CA 90723 (213) 531-1991

Morris Costume, 3108 Monroe Rd., Charlotte, NC 28205 (704) 332-3304

Morrissey Magic, 2882 Dufferin St., Toronto, Ontario, Canada M6B 3S6 (416)782-1393

If you want to stay in touch with jugglers and juggling, join the International Jugglers' Association (IJA). Membership brings you four issues of *Jugglers' World* magazine and a roster of members each year. Your IJA membership keeps you up to date on local juggling events and the annual IJA regional and national conventions. When you join the IJA, you will get a current list of prop makers who manufacture juggling equipment for professional performers and recreational jugglers. To inquire about current cost or to join, write to IJA, PO Box 3707JB, Akron, OH 44314-3704. After 5PM Eastern time or on weekends call (216) 745-3552 for membership information.

To network with jugglers and juggling in Europe, and to find out about the annual European Jugglers' Convention, subscribe to *Kaskade*. For subscription information, write to *Kaskade*, Annastrasse 7, D-6200, Wiesbaden, Germany.

To book jugglers or other variety entertainers for an event please contact Variety Plus, at (708) 766-3733 or The Jugglers Network at (212) 781-1440.

Lists of fairs and festivals around North America can be found in:

• *California Festivals, Festivals of the Pacific Northwest, Festivals of the Southwest, Festivals of New England,* all available from Landau Communications (415) 564-5689.

• *Chase's Annual Events*, a calendar of activities published annually by Contemporary Books, Chicago.

• *Directory of North American Fairs and Expositions*, published annually by Amusement Business, Box 24970, Nashville, TN 37202. (615) 321-4250

• *Festivals USA -- 1,000 Best Festivals by State and Region*, John Wiley, check for latest version.

To get in touch with the street scene and to stay up on the legal issues involved, write to Steven Baird, *The Street Performers' Newsletter*, PO Box 570, Cambridge, MA 02238-0570

To learn about the history of juggling and the life stories of the great jugglers of the past, the author recommends *Juggling - Its History and Greatest Performers*, by Francisco Alvarez, which presents a readable narrative and line drawings of some of the greats of the past. It is available from Francisco Alvarez, 220 Western Skies S.E. #1050, Albuquerque, NM 87123. Far more elaborate and more expensive is *Juggling, The Art and Its Artists*, by Karl Heinz Ziethen and Andrew Allen. This coffee-table book includes 290 black-and-white photographs, eight color plates and 93 drawings. The text is sparse and humorous. This book is published by Rausch and Luft, Hasenheide 54, D-1000, Berlin 61, West Germany.

If you would like to arrange for a speaker for associations or professional groups, using juggling as a medium for presenting a variety of messages, the following may be available:

• Having taught over a half million people to juggle, Dave Finnigan, AKA Professor Confidence, is not going to fail with your group. His program includes full participation by everyone in a joyous learning experience - (800) 523-1776.

• The humorous son of a humorist father, Steve Allen, Jr., M.D. incidentally teaches juggling as part of his program on the healing power of laughter and play - (607) 739-8778.

• Roni Lynn, O.T.R. specializes in groups that work with the elderly and disabled. She will help you to learn to use juggling as a playful form of therapy - (305) 966-3227

• Laurie Young and Kaye Kaskie through their workshop program entitled Laughter Works, present playshops using therapeutic juggling and other games with groups of all sorts throughout mid-America - (616) 624-5251

If you would like to learn how to present a professional quality instructional program in schools, recreation centers or other settings contact Mike Vondruska at The Illinois Juggling Institute - (800) 766-1437.

If you are interested in a summer camp that would deal exclusively in the art of juggling, please write to me care of JUGGLEBUG 7526J Olympic View Drive, Edmonds, WA 98026, (206) 774-2127.

Most importantly, keep juggling, keep learning new moves and teach this art to others. Together we can spread the joy of juggling throughout the known Universe.

For information on juggling workshops or performances, contact your nearest certified Juggling Institute instructor.

Pacific Northwest
Dave Finnigan, Juggling Inst., Edmonds, WA (800) 523-1776
Linda Severt, Juggletunes, Seattle, WA (206) 324-8251
Mag Hughes, We Care, West Linn, OR (503) 650-0858
Rocky Mountain States
Bruce Guettich, World Footbag, Golden, CO (303) 278-9797
California
Larry Kluger, N. Calif. J.I., Oakland, CA (415) 562-1212
Jahnathon Whitfield, Calif. J. I., Santa Ana, CA (714) 541-5845
Arizona/New Mexico
Robbie Weinstein, Flights of Fancy, Abq, NM (505) 266-9068
Texas
Tom Gear, Juggling for All, Houston, TX (713) 789-1906
Kent Cummins, Texas J. I., Austin, TX (512) 288-1596
Florida
Bob Goetzelman, Gulf Coast J.I., Ft. Meyer, FL (813) 267-7223
Roni Lynn, S. Fla. Jug. Acad., Hollywood, FL (305) 923-6070
Bruce Pfeffer, Circus of the Kids, Tallahasee, FL (904) 386-2685
Mid Atlantic
Don Fisher, DE Juggling Institute, Milford, DE (302) 422-7032
Benji Hill, J. I. of N. Virginia, Alexandria, VA (703) 971-6818
New Jersey & New York City
Charlie Carr, ACME J.I., North Plainfield, NJ (201) 754-1440
Philadelphia Area
Wayne Campbell, Levittown, PA (215) 946-6777
Al Angello, Norristown/Collegeville, PA (215) 489-7682
Hawaii
Graham Ellis, Hawaii Volcano Circus, Pahoa, HI (808) 965-8756
Sean Minnock, Maui, HI (808) 875-1234 ext. 4556
Ohio/Kentucky
Kevin Delagrange, N. Ohio J.I., Uniontown, OH (216) 896-1210
Tom Sparrough, Space Painter's J.I., Cincinatti, OH (513) 522-6776
Manitoba
Perry Rubenfeld, Cascade Juggling, Winnipeg, Man (204) 586-5785
Midwest and any areas not listed
Mike Vondruska, Illinois J.I., Bensenville, IL (708) 766-1437